Music Minus One
50 Executive Boulevard • Elmsford, New York 10523-1325
914-592-1188 • e-mail: info@musicminusone.com
www.musicminusone.com

Sing The Songs Of

Harry Warren

CONTENTS

©2014 MMO Music Group, Inc. All rights reserved.
ISBN 978-1-941566-14-5

MMO 2114

You'll Never Know

Words and Music by
Mack Gordon and Harry Warren

The More I See You

Words and Music by
Mack Gordon and Harry Warren

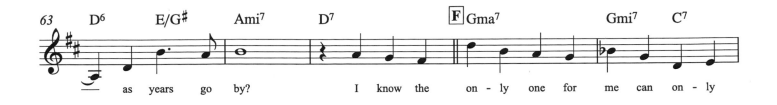

as years go by? I know the on-ly one for me can on-ly

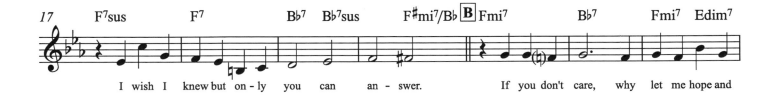

be you. My arms won't free you, my heart won't try.

I Wish I Knew

Words and Music by
Mack Gordon and Harry Warren

I wish I knew some-one like you could love me. I wish I

knew you place no one a-bove me. Did I mis-take this for a real ro-mance?

I wish I knew but on-ly you can an-swer. If you don't care, why let me hope and

pray so? Don't lead me on, if I'm a fool just say so. Should I keep dream-ing on, or

9

This Is Always

Words and Music by
Mack Gordon and Harry Warren

© 1946 (Renewed) WB MUSIC CORP.
This arrangement © 2014 WB MUSIC CORP.
All Rights Reserved Used by Permission
Reprinted by Permission of Hal Leonard Corporation

MMO 2114

10

MMO 2114

I Had The Craziest Dream

Words and Music by
Mack Gordon and Harry Warren

I Only Have Eyes For You

Words and Music by
Al Dubin and Harry Warren

Jeepers Creepers

Words and Music by
Johnny Mercer and Harry Warren

That's Amore

Words and Music by
Jack Brooks and Harry Warren

Serenade In Blue

Words and Music by
Mack Gordon and Harry Warren

Other Great Songs from this MMO Series

Vol. 1 - Sing the Songs of George & Ira Gershwin ....MMO 2101
Somebody Loves Me • The Man I Love • Bidin' My Time • Someone To Watch Over Me • I've Got A Crush On You • But Not For Me • S'Wonderful • Fascinatin' Rhythm

Vol. 2 - Sing the Songs of Cole Porter ....MMO 2102
Night And Day • You Do Something To Me • Just One Of Those Things • Begin The Beguine • What Is This Thing Called Love • Let's Do It • Love For Sale • I Get A Kick Out Of You

Vol. 3 - Sing the Songs of Irving Berlin ....MMO 2103
Cheek To Cheek • Steppin' Out With My Baby • Let's Face The Music And Dance • Change Partners • Let Yourself Go • Say It Isn't So • Isn't This A Lovely Day • This Year's Kisses • Be Careful, It's My Heart

Vol. 4 - Sing the Songs of Harold Arlen ....MMO 2104
I've Got The World On A String • Down With Love • As Long As I Live • Stormy Weather • I've Got A Right To Sing The Blues • The Blues In The Night • Out Of This World • Come Rain Or Come Shine • My Shining Hour • Hooray For Love

Vol. 5 - Sing More Songs by George & Ira Gershwin, Vol. 2 ....MMO 2105
Of Thee I Sing • Embraceable You • Oh, Lady Be Good • How Long Has This Been Going On? • Summertime • Love Walked In • Nice Work If You Can Get It • I Got Rhythm

Vol. 6 - Sing the Songs of Duke Ellington ....MMO 2106
Do Nothin' Until You Hear From Me • I Got It Bad (And That Ain't Good) • I Let A Song Go Out Of My Heart • It Don't Mean A Thing (If It Ain't Got That Swing) • Mood Indigo • Solitude • Sophisticated Lady • Don't Get Around Much Anymore

Vol. 7 - Sing the Songs of Fats Waller ....MMO 2107
I'm Gonna Sit Right Down And Write Myself A Letter • I've Got A Feeling I'm Falling • Squeeze Me • S'posin' • Two Sleepy People • Ain't Misbehavin' (I'm Savin' My Love For You) • Honeysuckle Rose • I Can't Give You Anything But Love • It's A Sin To Tell A Lie

Vol. 8 - Sing the Songs of Cole Porter, Vol. 2 ....MMO 2108
You're The Top • Easy To Love • Friendship • Anything Goes • Blow, Gabriel, Blow • You're The Top (Jazz Version) • I Get A Kick Out Of You • Anything Goes (Jazz Version)

Vol. 9 - Sing the Songs of Jimmy McHugh ....MMO 2109
It's A Most Unusual Day • You're a Sweetheart • Don't Blame Me • I Feel A Song Coming On • I'm in the Mood for Love • I Can't Give You Anything But Love • I Can't Believe That You're in Love with Me • On the Sunny Side of the Street • I Must Have That Man

Vol. 10 - Sing the Songs of Jerome Kern ....MMO 2110
A Fine Romance • Smoke Gets In Your Eyes • The Last Time I Saw Paris • The Way You Look Tonight • Yesterdays • The Folks Who Live On The Hill • Make Believe • I'm Old Fashioned • All The Things You Are • They Didn't Believe Me

Vol. 11 - Sing the Songs of Johnny Mercer ....MMO 2111
Come Rain or Come Shine • Charade • The Days of Wine and Roses • Dream • I'm Old Fashioned • I Wanna Be Around • Jeepers Creepers • Moon River • One For My Baby

Vol. 12 - Sing the Songs of Johnny Mercer, Vol. 2 ....MMO 2112
The Autumn Leaves • Fools Rush In • I Remember You • My Shining Hour • Skylark • Tangerine • Too Marvelous For Words • Mr. Meadowlark

Vol. 13 - Sing the Songs of Rodgers & Hart ....MMO 2113
I Didn't Know What Time It Was • My Funny Valentine • Nobody's Heart Belongs To Me • A Ship Without A Sail • Dancing On The Ceiling • It Never Entered My Mind • There's A Small Hotel • Where Or When

Vol. 14 - Sing the Songs of Harry Warren ....MMO 2114
You'll Never Know • The More I See You • I Wish I Knew • This Is Always • I Had The Craziest Dream • I Only Have Eyes For You • Jeepers Creepers • That's Amore • Serenade In Blue

Music Minus One
50 Executive Boulevard • Elmsford, New York 10523-1325
914-592-1188 • e-mail: info@musicminusone.com
www.musicminusone.com

MMO 2114

ISBN 978-1-941566-14-5